I0192069

Courage to Soar

A Graduate's 52 Week Devotional

For Bulk Order requests email: contact@adventuresofpookie.com

Printed in the United States of America
Paperback ISBN : 979-8-9988824-2-5
Hardcover ISBN: 979-8-9988824-3-2

www.AdventuresOfPookie.com

Dedication

To my nieces and nephews. The ones who have my whole heart.

Your life is the most precious thing to me. Watching you grow from a child to the person you are today, has given me such happiness and joy.

Every day I pray that you wake up and know that you are loved, you are wanted, and you are special. Every day I pray that you look in the mirror and know that you are fearfully and wonderfully made and that you are perfect as you are. Every day I pray that you follow your heart. To know that your dreams and passions matter. To know that your purpose, no matter what dream you pursue, is to bring all of the love, kindness, and joy to this world as you have brought to me. Every day I pray that God will fill you with all joy and peace as you trust in him, so that you may overflow with hope.

Life is not always fair or easy, but life is always worth it. Life is a gift that you were given and your life means something. To live is the greatest adventure of all.

My dream for you is to become the person you are meant to be. My dream is for you to see the world and conquer it. My dream for you is to never give up and always push forward.

I want to leave you with one of my favorite verses:

"Be strong and courageous. Do not be afraid; do not be discouraged, for the Lord your God will be with you wherever you go." – Joshua 1:9. This verse has guided me to be the best version of myself because I know the Lord is with me.

I wish this for you. I wish this for you because though I am always here for you, I will not always be on earth to remind you, but God will always be there for you. Never forget that. Never forget you matter. Never forget you are special. You are precious. And you are loved.

With all my heart has to give,
Love your Aunt Rebecca 🤍

Introduction

YOU DID IT!

You've crossed the stage, turned your tassel, and stepped into a new chapter filled with possibility, excitement, and, let's be honest—some uncertainty too.

Graduation is more than a ceremony. It's a launching point. A moment where one season ends and another begins. Whether you feel completely ready or totally unsure, know this: God is with you, and He has a plan for your life that's bigger and better than anything you can imagine.

Courage to Soar was created just for you—a 52-week devotional designed to help you stay grounded in God's truth as you navigate the year ahead. Each week, you'll find a short devotional focused on real-life topics: identity, purpose, fear, failure, relationships, decisions, and more. Every entry includes a Bible verse, a devotional thought, reflection questions, and a prayer to help you walk closer with God.

Why "courage to soar"?

Because stepping into adulthood takes bravery. Following Jesus in a world full of noise and pressure takes strength. But when your courage comes from Christ, you won't just survive—you'll soar. Not because life will be easy, but because the One who leads you is faithful.

You don't have to have it all figured out. You just need to keep showing up. Keep seeking Him. And keep trusting that God is writing a story with your life that is full of purpose, beauty, and impact.

So take a breath. Open your heart. Let's walk this journey together—one week at a time.

YOU'VE GOT THIS.

And more importantly, GOD'S GOT YOU.

The Launchpad of Faith

SCRIPTURE

"Have I not commanded you? Be strong and courageous. Do not be afraid; do not be discouraged, for the Lord your God will be with you wherever you go." — Joshua 1:9 (NIV)

DEVOTIONAL

Graduation is more than a ceremony—it's a launchpad. You've reached a milestone that took effort, endurance, and probably more late nights than you care to count. Now, a wide-open sky stretches before you, full of possibility—and uncertainty.

God's words to Joshua still echo for every graduate standing on the edge of a new beginning: Be strong. Be courageous. As you step into the unknown—whether it's college, a career, or something entirely different—remember that courage doesn't mean having all the answers. It means trusting the One who does.

Just like Joshua stepping into the Promised Land, your journey may be filled with both opportunity and challenge. But God's promise is the same: *I will be with you wherever you go.*

PRAYER

Father, thank You for bringing me to this point. As I step into what's next, help me to walk with courage, not fear. Remind me that You are with me in every unknown. Give me strength, wisdom, and peace as I soar into this new season. Amen.

REFLECTION

What fears or uncertainties are you carrying about the future? How can you invite God into those areas today? In what ways has He already shown His faithfulness in your life?

_____

_____

_____

_____

_____

_____

_____

_____

_____

_____

_____

Trusting the Mapmaker

SCRIPTURE

'For I know the plans I have for you,' declares the
Lord, 'plans to prosper you and not to harm you,
plans to give you a hope and a future.'
— Jeremiah 29:11 (NIV)

DEVOTIONAL

Graduation often brings big questions: What's
next? Did I make the right decision? Will things work
out? It's easy to feel pressure to have your whole life
figured out at eighteen.

But God isn't asking you to have it all planned—
He's asking you to trust that He does. Like a skilled
mapmaker, He sees every turn ahead. Your job isn't
to guess the route—it's to stay close to the Guide.

Even when the path is unclear, your future
is not uncertain to God. His plans are good. Not
always easy, not always predictable—but good.

PRAYER

God, sometimes I feel overwhelmed by all the decisions in front of me. Help me remember that I don't have to figure everything out. Teach me to trust You with each step. Thank You for having a plan and purpose for my life. Amen.

REFLECTION

Are you placing more pressure on yourself to figure things out than God is? What would it look like to trust Him with your next step instead of your whole future? How has God shown His faithfulness in past seasons?

_____

_____

_____

_____

_____

_____

_____

_____

_____

_____

Fear Has No Place Here

SCRIPTURE

"For God has not given us a spirit of fear, but of power and of love and of a sound mind."
— 2 Timothy 1:7 (NKJV)

DEVOTIONAL

Fear sneaks in quietly—before the job interview, the first college class, or moving away from home. But fear isn't from God. He doesn't lead through fear. He leads with peace, courage, and clarity.

When fear shows up, remind it who you belong to. God has given you power to stand firm, love to steady your heart, and a sound mind to make wise decisions. Fear might knock, but it doesn't have to live with you.

Courage doesn't mean you never feel afraid. It means fear doesn't get the final say.

PRAYER

Lord, fear feels real and heavy sometimes. But I know You didn't give it to me. Help me walk in the power, love, and sound mind that come from You. I choose courage over fear today. Amen.

REFLECTION

What specific fears are you facing right now? How can you speak truth over those fears? Who can you talk to for encouragement and prayer?

_____

_____

_____

_____

_____

_____

_____

_____

_____

_____

_____

_____

Ask for Wisdom

SCRIPTURE

"If any of you lacks wisdom, you should ask God, who gives generously to all without finding fault, and it will be given to you." — James 1:5 (NIV)

DEVOTIONAL

The world is full of voices telling you what to do, who to be, and where to go. But wisdom isn't just knowledge—it's knowing how to live well, how to make choices that honor God and serve others.

And here's the amazing part: God wants to give you wisdom. He's not stingy or silent. When you don't know what to do next, ask Him. He's not disappointed in your questions—He delights in your dependence.

So before you Google it, guess, or go with the crowd—pause and pray. Ask the One who knows everything to guide you.

PRAYER

Father, I need Your wisdom. Not just information, but understanding. Help me to seek Your voice above the noise and trust that You will lead me in the right direction. Amen.

REFLECTION

Where do you need wisdom right now? Are you turning to God first, or as a last resort? What's one decision you can pray over today?

_____

_____

_____

_____

_____

_____

_____

_____

_____

_____

_____

Who Am I, Really?

SCRIPTURE

"I have been crucified with Christ and I no longer live, but Christ lives in me..." — Galatians 2:20 (NIV)

DEVOTIONAL

Your achievements don't define you. Neither do your grades, your popularity, or your future plans. Your identity is not earned—it's given. You are who God says you are: loved, chosen, redeemed, and made new in Christ.

When the world tries to label you, remember who you already are. You are not just a graduate. You are a child of God.

Live from that identity—not trying to prove your worth, but secure in it. That kind of confidence isn't arrogance—it's freedom.

PRAYER

Jesus, thank You for defining who I am. Help me not to get caught up in labels or achievements, but to remember that my identity is secure in You. Remind me daily that I am Yours. Amen.

REFLECTION

What voices try to define your worth? How can you root your identity deeper in Christ? What changes when you live from a place of security instead of striving?

_____

_____

_____

_____

_____

_____

_____

_____

_____

_____

_____

_____

_____

_____

_____

Strength in the Struggle

SCRIPTURE

"...we also glory in our sufferings, because we know that suffering produces perseverance; perseverance, character; and character, hope."
— Romans 5:3-4 (NIV)

DEVOTIONAL

Hard things don't mean you're doing something wrong. They often mean you're growing. Struggles stretch us. They teach us perseverance. They shape our character. And they ultimately anchor our hope—not in a perfect life, but in a faithful God.

This new season may include challenges you didn't expect. That's okay. Struggles don't cancel God's promises—they prepare you for them.

Let your hardships be holy ground. He's working even in the waiting, even in the difficulty.

PRAYER

God, I don't always understand why things are hard, but I trust You are working in and through every challenge. Give me strength to persevere and hope that does not disappoint. Amen.

REFLECTION

What recent struggles have stretched your faith? How has God used hard times to grow your character? What can you thank Him for, even in difficulty?

_____

_____

_____

_____

_____

_____

_____

_____

_____

_____

_____

_____

_____

_____

_____

Gratitude Changes Everything

SCRIPTURE

"Give thanks in all circumstances; for this is God's will for you in Christ Jesus."
— 1 Thessalonians 5:18 (NIV)

DEVOTIONAL

Gratitude isn't just for good days. It's a daily choice that shifts your perspective. In a world that moves fast and often feels demanding, pausing to give thanks slows your heart and realigns it with God. It reminds you that even in uncertainty, you are blessed.

Gratitude isn't about pretending everything is perfect—it's about seeing God's hand even in the imperfect. When you choose to give thanks, even in small things, you open the door to deeper joy.

PRAYER

Lord, thank You for the many gifts in my life. Help me to see Your goodness even in challenges. Give me a heart that is quick to thank You and slow to complain. Amen.

REFLECTION

What are three things you can thank God for today? How does gratitude affect your attitude toward difficult situations? When is it hardest for you to be thankful?

_____

_____

_____

_____

_____

_____

_____

_____

_____

_____

_____

_____

_____

_____

_____

Choose Your Circle

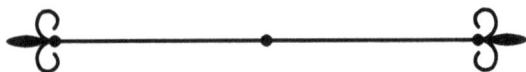

SCRIPTURE

"Walk with the wise and become wise, for a companion of fools suffers harm."
— Proverbs 13:20 (NIV)

DEVOTIONAL

The people you surround yourself with shape your future more than you might realize. In this new season, you'll meet lots of new people—some will build you up, others may pull you down.
God designed us for community, but not all community is healthy. Choose friends who inspire your faith, encourage your growth, and challenge you to be your best. You become like those you spend the most time with.

Don't be afraid to set boundaries or walk away from relationships that lead you away from God's best. True friends won't compete with your calling— they'll celebrate it. The right people will remind you who you are and point you back to who God is.

PRAYER

Father, guide me to friendships that honor You. Give me discernment to know which relationships to pursue and which to step back from. Help me be a light in my friendships. Amen.

REFLECTION

Who in your life encourages you to follow Jesus? Are there relationships you need to set boundaries in? How can you be a wise and godly friend to others?

_____

_____

_____

_____

_____

_____

_____

_____

_____

_____

_____

Step Out of the Boat

SCRIPTURE

"'Come,' he said. Then Peter got down out of the boat, walked on the water and came toward Jesus."
— Matthew 14:29 (NIV)

DEVOTIONAL

Stepping into the unknown takes faith. Peter had to step out of the boat before he could walk on water. You may be standing at the edge of something new, and fear might be whispering, What if I sink? But Jesus is calling you to more. He doesn't promise the water won't be rough, but He does promise to meet you there. The safest place to be is wherever Jesus is—yes, even on the waves.

Courage doesn't mean you won't feel afraid; it means you move forward anyway, trusting that Jesus is greater than the storm. The miracle didn't happen in the comfort of the boat—it happened in the risk of the step.

So take the step. Fix your eyes on Him. That's where faith begins—and where the impossible becomes possible.

PRAYER

Jesus, I want to follow You, even when I'm afraid. Help me to keep my eyes on You and not on the wind and waves around me. Give me faith to step out boldly. Amen.

REFLECTION

What is one step of faith you feel God is calling you to take? What's holding you back from stepping out? How can you focus more on Jesus than on the waves?

_____

_____

_____

_____

_____

_____

_____

_____

_____

_____

_____

Lean Not on Your Own Understanding

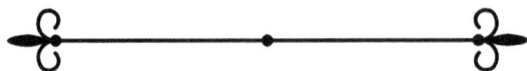

SCRIPTURE

"Trust in the Lord with all your heart and lean not on your own understanding; in all your ways submit to him, and he will make your paths straight."
— Proverbs 3:5–6 (NIV)

DEVOTIONAL

You don't have to have it all figured out. In fact, trusting God means acknowledging that you don't. Leaning on your own understanding might feel safer, but it's limited.

God sees the full picture—every detour, every delay, every door that opens or shuts. Your job is to trust, not to control. Let His wisdom guide you, even when it doesn't make sense yet.

Sometimes, the most powerful thing you can do is take the next step in faith, even without a full map. His timing is perfect, His ways are higher, and His plans are always for your good.

When you release the need to know everything, you make room for peace to grow. God's direction may not always be clear, but His presence will never leave you.

PRAYER

God, I confess that I often lean on my own understanding. Help me to trust You with all my heart. Guide my steps and help me to follow even when I don't see the full path. Amen.

REFLECTION

What area of your life are you trying to control right now? What would it look like to fully trust God in that area? Can you remember a time when God led you in an unexpected but better direction?

_____

_____

_____

_____

_____

_____

_____

_____

_____

_____

Discipline Is Not a Dirty Word

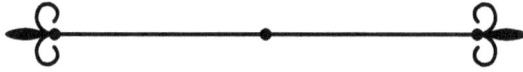

SCRIPTURE

"No discipline seems pleasant at the time, but painful. Later on, however, it produces a harvest of righteousness and peace..." — Hebrews 12:11 (NIV)

DEVOTIONAL

Discipline isn't fun—but it's worth it. Waking up early to study, staying true to your values, showing up consistently... these choices build strength over time.

God disciplines not to punish but to shape us. In a world that prioritizes ease, you're called to choose the harder—but better—path. Small daily decisions lead to long-term faithfulness.

Discipline is like training for a race—you may not see results right away, but every step matters. It develops endurance, character, and spiritual grit. When no one is watching, when it's inconvenient, when quitting would be easier—that's when discipline turns into devotion. Keep showing up. God is doing more in your obedience than you can see right now.

PRAYER

Lord, help me not to run from discipline but to embrace it. Teach me the value of faithfulness in the little things. Grow my character so I can be more like You. Amen.

REFLECTION

What areas of your life need more discipline? How can you invite God into your habits and routines? What "harvest" do you hope to see from your current efforts?

_____

_____

_____

_____

_____

_____

_____

_____

_____

_____

In His Time

SCRIPTURE

"There is a time for everything, and a season for every activity under the heavens."
— Ecclesiastes 3:1 (NIV)

DEVOTIONAL

God's timing rarely matches ours. We want things now—answers, opportunities, breakthroughs. But God moves with purpose, not pressure.

Waiting is not wasted. It's where trust grows. When doors don't open as quickly as you hoped, remember: delays are not denials. Your story is unfolding in exactly the right time.

In the waiting, God is preparing you for what He's prepared for you. He's working behind the scenes, shaping your heart, building your character, and aligning the details.

So don't rush what God is writing. The best things often take time—and His timing is never late. Keep showing up. Keep trusting. What feels like a pause may actually be part of your breakthrough.

PRAYER

Father, waiting is hard. Help me to be patient and trust that Your timing is best. Give me peace in the waiting and faith that You are working. Amen.

REFLECTION

Are you in a season of waiting right now? How can you make the most of this season instead of rushing through it? What is one thing God might be teaching you while you wait?

_____

_____

_____

_____

_____

_____

_____

_____

_____

_____

_____

_____

Live to Serve

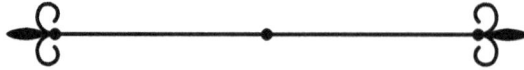

SCRIPTURE

"For even the Son of Man did not come to be served, but to serve…" — Mark 10:45 (NIV)

DEVOTIONAL

Success in God's Kingdom doesn't come from being first—but from putting others first. Jesus, the King of kings, chose the role of servant.

You don't need a title to make a difference. You just need a heart willing to serve. Look around—there's always someone who needs encouragement, help, or kindness. You are never more like Jesus than when you serve.

In a world chasing influence, choose impact. True leadership starts with humility. Whether it's holding a door, listening to a friend, or showing up when it's inconvenient—those small acts echo in eternity.

Greatness in God's eyes looks like love in action. Serve where you are, with what you have. It matters more than you know.

PRAYER

Jesus, thank You for modeling what it means to serve. Help me to follow Your example. Open my eyes to the needs around me and give me a willing heart to serve with love. Amen.

REFLECTION

What opportunities to serve are right in front of you? Do you see service as something optional or essential? How does serving others shape your character?

_____

_____

_____

_____

_____

_____

_____

_____

_____

_____

_____

Guard Your Heart

SCRIPTURE

"Above all else, guard your heart, for everything you do flows from it." — Proverbs 4:23 (NIV)

DEVOTIONAL

Your heart is valuable—what you allow in will shape your thoughts, your choices, and your future. That's why Scripture urges you to guard it, not casually, but *above all else*.

Be mindful of what you watch, listen to, and surround yourself with. Guarding your heart doesn't mean hiding it. It means protecting what God is doing in you so it can flourish.

You are constantly being influenced—by media, conversations, relationships, and even your inner dialogue. Choose wisely what you let take root.

A guarded heart isn't a closed one—it's a heart that stays open to God and closed to compromise. Protect it like the treasure it is, because from it flows the direction of your life.

PRAYER

Lord, help me to guard my heart with wisdom. Show me anything that's pulling me away from You and give me strength to let it go. Help me protect what You are growing in me. Amen.

REFLECTION

What things are influencing your heart right now? Are there habits or influences you need to limit or remove? What practices help you keep your heart aligned with God?

_____

_____

_____

_____

_____

_____

_____

_____

_____

_____

_____

Integrity Matters

SCRIPTURE

"Whoever walks in integrity walks securely…"
— Proverbs 10:9 (NIV)

DEVOTIONAL

In a world full of shortcuts and cover-ups, integrity stands out. It means doing what's right even when no one's watching.

Walking with integrity won't always be the easiest path, but it will always be the most secure. Your reputation can open doors—but your character determines how long you stay there. Live in a way that honors God, even when it's hard.

Integrity is who you are when no one's looking and what you choose when no one will ever know. It's built in quiet moments and tested in pressure.

Don't trade long-term peace for short-term gain. When you live with integrity, you can walk in confidence—knowing you've chosen what's right, even when it costs something.

PRAYER

God, help me to live with integrity in all areas of my life. Give me courage to choose honesty, purity, and faithfulness even when it's difficult. Let my life reflect You. Amen.

REFLECTION

Where in your life is integrity being tested? What would it look like to choose what's right over what's easy? Who in your life models integrity well?

_____

_____

_____

_____

_____

_____

_____

_____

_____

_____

_____

Give It Your Best

SCRIPTURE

"Whatever you do, work at it with all your heart, as working for the Lord, not for human masters."
— Colossians 3:23 (NIV)

DEVOTIONAL

Whatever season you're in—whether it's college, work, or something else—do it with excellence. Not for applause, not for status, but for God.

He sees every quiet act of faithfulness. Your work, your studies, your efforts—they all become worship when offered to Him. Excellence isn't perfection—it's giving your best because He deserves your best.

Even the ordinary moments matter. God can use your diligence in the small things to prepare you for greater things ahead.

So show up. Give your all. And remember—when you work for God, nothing is wasted. He is honored in your effort, not just your outcomes.

PRAYER

Lord, help me to work with excellence in all I do. Remind me that I'm ultimately working for You, not for recognition or reward. Let my work reflect my love for You. Amen.

REFLECTION

What motivates you to give your best effort? Is there an area where you've been tempted to coast or quit? How can you shift your mindset to work as worship?

_____

_____

_____

_____

_____

_____

_____

_____

_____

_____

_____

You Are Not Alone

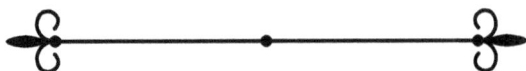

SCRIPTURE

"Never will I leave you; never will I forsake you."
— Hebrews 13:5b (NIV)

DEVOTIONAL

New seasons can feel lonely—new places, new faces, unfamiliar routines. But you are never truly alone. God's presence goes with you. His promise isn't just for when you feel close to Him. It stands even in the silence.

When friends feel distant or you're unsure who to turn to, turn to the One who has never left your side.

He sees every tear, hears every unspoken prayer, and walks with you even when no one else does. Loneliness may visit, but it doesn't have to stay—because the God who loves you is near.

Lean into His presence. Let Him fill the empty spaces. His companionship is constant, and His love never fades.

PRAYER

Lord, thank You for always being with me. When I feel alone, remind me of Your nearness. Help me rest in the promise that You never leave or forsake me. Amen.

REFLECTION

When have you felt most alone, and how did God show up for you? How can you remind yourself of God's presence during hard days? What habits help you stay connected to Him?

_____

_____

_____

_____

_____

_____

_____

_____

_____

_____

When You Feel Inadequate

SCRIPTURE

"My grace is sufficient for you, for my power is made perfect in weakness." — 2 Corinthians 12:9a (NIV)

DEVOTIONAL

Feelings of inadequacy are normal when stepping into something new. But you're not expected to have all the answers. God doesn't call the equipped—He equips the called.

His grace fills the gaps where your strength ends. You're not too young, too inexperienced, or too unsure for Him to use you. In fact, those are often the very qualities He uses to reveal His power.

Remember, your limitations create space for God's strength to shine the brightest. Trust that He is working in and through you, preparing you for every step ahead.

Step forward with confidence—not in yourself, but in the One who called you. Your "not enough" is where His "more than enough" begins.

PRAYER

Father, I admit I sometimes feel like I'm not enough. But thank You that Your grace is. Use my weaknesses to show Your strength. I trust You to work through me. Amen.

REFLECTION

What makes you feel inadequate or unqualified? How does God's grace give you confidence in those areas? Can you think of a time when God worked through your weakness?

_____

_____

_____

_____

_____

_____

_____

_____

_____

_____

The Power of Your Words

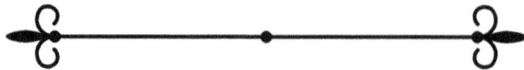

SCRIPTURE

"The tongue has the power of life and death…"
— Proverbs 18:21a (NIV)

DEVOTIONAL

Words matter. They can lift someone up or tear them down in seconds. In a world where comments fly quickly and criticism is common, your words can be a light.

Use your voice to encourage, not just to express opinions. Speak truth, but speak it in love. The way you speak reveals the heart behind it. Choose words that reflect Jesus.

Remember, words have power—not just to change situations, but to shape minds and hearts, including your own.

Before you speak, pause and ask: *Will this build up or break down? Will this reflect God's love or fuel division?*

Let your speech be seasoned with grace, kindness, and hope—because your words can plant seeds that grow far beyond what you see.

PRAYER

Lord, help me to speak words that bring life. Teach me to think before I speak and to let kindness guide my conversations. Use my voice to reflect Your heart. Amen.

REFLECTION

Are your words building people up or tearing them down? How can you be more intentional with your speech this week? What's one way to use your words to encourage someone today?

_____

_____

_____

_____

_____

_____

_____

_____

_____

_____

The Purpose in Pain

SCRIPTURE

"And we know that in all things God works for the good of those who love him..." — Romans 8:28a (NIV)

DEVOTIONAL

Pain isn't pointless. God doesn't cause all the hard things, but He promises to use them. Every disappointment, detour, and heartbreak can become part of something redemptive in His hands. It may not make sense now, but you're being shaped through it. Trust that even when you can't see the purpose, God is still at work.

Sometimes, the strongest faith is forged in the fire of hardship. Your struggles don't define you—they refine you.

Hold on to hope, knowing that God's love is greater than your pain, and His plans for you are filled with restoration and new beginnings.

PRAYER

God, help me trust You in the hard times. I may not understand the "why," but I believe You are good and working all things for good. Use my pain to shape my purpose. Amen.

REFLECTION

What painful experience has God used to grow you? How does knowing God is working for your good change how you face hardship? What's one truth you can hold onto in your current struggle?

_____

_____

_____

_____

_____

_____

_____

_____

_____

_____

Light in the Darkness

SCRIPTURE

"You are the light of the world. A town built on a hill cannot be hidden." — Matthew 5:14 (NIV)

DEVOTIONAL

You were created to shine—not just when it's easy, but especially when it's dark. Light isn't loud, but it is noticeable. It doesn't argue with the dark. It simply shows up.

As a graduate stepping into the world, you have an opportunity to be a reflection of Christ. Let your kindness, faith, and love stand out—not for applause, but to point others to Him.

Sometimes the world feels heavy and dark, but your light can be the hope someone desperately needs.

Don't underestimate the power of a gentle word, a patient heart, or a consistent witness. Your quiet light can break through the shadows and remind others that God's love is real and present.

PRAYER

Jesus, help me be a light in a world that desperately needs You. Let my life point others to Your hope and truth. Teach me to shine with courage and compassion. Amen.

REFLECTION

Where is God calling you to be a light? Are you trying to blend in when you were made to stand out? How can your daily actions reflect God's love?

_____

_____

_____

_____

_____

_____

_____

_____

_____

_____

_____

_____

Stay Planted

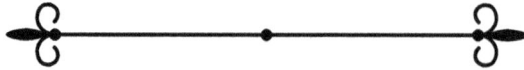

SCRIPTURE

"Blessed is the one... whose delight is in the law of the Lord... That person is like a tree planted by streams of water..." — Psalm 1:1–3 (NIV)

DEVOTIONAL

Growth comes when you stay rooted. In a season full of movement and change, your soul needs something steady. That's God's Word.

When you're planted in truth, you'll have strength in every season—good or bad. You won't dry up in hard times. You'll bear fruit. Stay close to the source.

Just like a tree draws nourishment from deep roots, your spirit draws life from God's promises. The deeper you dig into His Word, the more resilient and vibrant you become.

No matter how strong the winds of change blow, the roots of your faith will hold you firm. Keep watering your soul with Scripture, prayer, and worship—these are the lifelines that keep you growing.

PRAYER

Lord, help me stay rooted in You. Let Your Word nourish my heart and guide my steps. Teach me to grow deep before I try to grow wide. Amen.

REFLECTION

What spiritual practices help you stay rooted in God? Have you been feeling spiritually dry? What could help refresh you? How do you make space for God's Word in your routine?

_____

_____

_____

_____

_____

_____

_____

_____

_____

_____

_____

_____

Failure Isn't Final

SCRIPTURE

"Though the righteous fall seven times, they rise again..." — Proverbs 24:16a (NIV)

DEVOTIONAL

Failure doesn't define you—getting back up does. Everyone stumbles. The key is refusing to stay down.

God's grace gives you the strength to start again. Failure is a teacher, not a label. Don't let it keep you from pursuing your calling. God isn't finished with you.

Each setback is a stepping stone, an opportunity to learn, grow, and come back stronger. What feels like an end can be the beginning of something greater.

Remember, some of the greatest stories in the Bible are filled with people who failed but didn't give up—because God's power is made perfect in weakness.

So rise with courage, knowing that your worth isn't measured by your mistakes, but by God's unending love and the hope He has for your future.

PRAYER

God, thank You for not giving up on me when I fall.
Help me to rise again with Your strength. Teach me
through my failures and grow my faith through them.
Amen.

REFLECTION

How do you usually respond to failure? What has
failure taught you about resilience or dependence
on God? Is there an area where God is inviting you to
try again?

_____

_____

_____

_____

_____

_____

_____

_____

_____

_____

Keep First Things First

SCRIPTURE

"But seek first his kingdom and his righteousness, and all these things will be given to you as well."
— Matthew 6:33 (NIV)

DEVOTIONAL

Life is full of demands—assignments, jobs, relationships, goals. But when everything feels urgent, remember what's important: seeking God first.

When you put Him first, everything else finds its right place. He isn't just another item on your to-do list. He's the foundation your whole life rests on. It's easy to get caught up in the rush, trying to juggle everything at once, but true peace and balance come when your heart is anchored in Him.

Prioritizing God doesn't mean ignoring responsibilities—it means trusting Him to guide your steps and give you strength for each day.

When He is your first focus, your decisions become clearer, your worries lighter, and your purpose more aligned with His perfect plan.

PRAYER

Father, help me to seek You above everything else. Teach me to order my life around You, not just fit You in. Let Your priorities become mine. Amen.

REFLECTION

What does it look like to seek God first in your daily routine? What things tend to crowd out time with Him? How have you seen God provide when you've prioritized Him?

_____

_____

_____

_____

_____

_____

_____

_____

_____

_____

_____

You Are God's Masterpiece

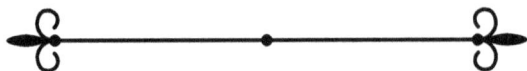

SCRIPTURE

"For we are God's handiwork, created in Christ Jesus to do good works..." — Ephesians 2:10 (NIV)

DEVOTIONAL

You weren't an accident. You were designed with care, intention, and purpose. You are God's masterpiece.

There's something only you can do. There are good works prepared for you—opportunities to love, lead, create, and serve that fit your gifts and personality. Embrace who you are in Him.

No one else can fulfill the unique role God has for you. Your story, your talents, and your passions are all part of His divine plan.

When you step into who God created you to be, you'll find fulfillment and joy that nothing else can provide. Trust that He made you perfectly for this time and place.

Celebrate your uniqueness, and don't compare your journey to anyone else's. You were made to shine in your own way.

PRAYER

God, thank You for creating me with purpose. Help me to see myself the way You see me. Show me the good works You've prepared for me, and give me courage to walk in them. Amen.

REFLECTION

What are some ways God has uniquely gifted you? Do you believe you're His masterpiece, or do you struggle with that truth? How can you use your gifts to impact the world?

_____

_____

_____

_____

_____

_____

_____

_____

_____

_____

_____

Small Steps Matter

SCRIPTURE

"Do not despise these small beginnings, for the Lord rejoices to see the work begin…"
— Zechariah 4:10a (NLT)

DEVOTIONAL

Big dreams often start with small steps. You don't have to have everything figured out to move forward. God celebrates progress, not perfection.

Don't underestimate the power of showing up, staying faithful, and doing the next right thing. Over time, those small steps become a God-sized story.

Sometimes the path feels uncertain, and the destination seems far away—but every small step you take is a step toward the future God has planned.

Trust that He honors your faithfulness, no matter how small the action. Your consistent efforts are building something greater than you can see right now.

Keep moving forward with hope and courage, knowing that God is with you in every step of the journey.

PRAYER

Lord, thank You that You delight in small beginnings. Help me not to wait for perfect conditions but to start where I am. Let my small steps honor You. Amen.

REFLECTION

What small beginning are you in right now? Have you been waiting for something "big" before you take a step? How can you stay faithful in the little things?

_____

_____

_____

_____

_____

_____

_____

_____

_____

_____

_____

Guard Your Heart

SCRIPTURE

"Above all else, guard your heart, for everything you do flows from it." — Proverbs 4:23 (NIV)

DEVOTIONAL

Your heart is the wellspring of your life—it's where your values, dreams, and emotions live. And it's also where the enemy tries to sneak in lies, bitterness, and fear.

Be intentional about what you allow in. Your influences—music, media, friendships, even your thoughts—affect the health of your heart. Guard it, not with fear, but with wisdom.

Just as a garden needs careful tending to grow strong and beautiful, your heart needs protection and nourishment to thrive.

Choose to fill it with truth, love, and encouragement, and be quick to remove anything that threatens to choke out your faith and joy.

Remember, what you guard today shapes the life you live tomorrow. Keep your heart focused on God, the source of all hope and peace.

PRAYER

Lord, teach me to guard my heart with discernment. Show me what to let in and what to let go of. Help me fill my heart with Your truth and love. Amen.

REFLECTION

What has the most influence on your heart right now? Are there things you need to limit or remove to protect your heart? How can you feed your heart with truth?

_____

_____

_____

_____

_____

_____

_____

_____

_____

_____

_____

Living with Integrity

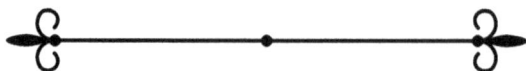

SCRIPTURE

"The integrity of the upright guides them, but the unfaithful are destroyed by their duplicity."
— Proverbs 11:3 (NIV)

DEVOTIONAL

Integrity is doing the right thing even when no one is watching. It's choosing honesty, even when it's uncomfortable. In a world full of shortcuts and double standards, integrity sets you apart.

As you step into new freedoms and responsibilities, let your choices reflect your character—not your circumstances.

Integrity isn't always the easiest path, but it's the one that leads to true respect and lasting peace. It builds trust with others and strengthens your relationship with God.

Remember, your reputation might open doors, but your integrity determines how long you stay. Make decisions that honor God, even when it costs you something.

Living with integrity means your "yes" means yes, and your "no" means no. It's being consistent in who you are—because your character is your greatest testimony.

PRAYER

God, help me live with integrity in every area of my life. Give me courage to do what's right even when it's hard. Let my character reflect Yours. Amen.

REFLECTION

What does integrity look like in your current stage of life? Are there areas where it's hard to be honest or consistent? Who in your life models integrity well?

_____

_____

_____

_____

_____

_____

_____

_____

_____

_____

_____

God Goes Before You

SCRIPTURE

"The Lord himself goes before you and will be with you..." — Deuteronomy 31:8a (NIV)

DEVOTIONAL

You don't step into the unknown alone—God goes before you. He's already in your future, preparing the path and the people, opening doors and closing others for your good.

Even when things feel uncertain, you can move forward with confidence, knowing He's one step ahead, guiding your way.

God's plans are always for your good and His glory, even when they don't match your timeline or expectations.

Trust that He is orchestrating every detail, often in ways you can't yet see or understand.

So step boldly into the new season—fearless, knowing that the Creator of the universe is lighting your path and walking right beside you every step of the way.

PRAYER

Lord, thank You for going before me. Help me to trust You with the unknown and walk forward in faith, knowing You are already there. Amen.

REFLECTION

What unknowns are making you anxious right now? How can the truth that God goes before you give you peace? Have you seen God prepare the way for you in the past?

_____

_____

_____

_____

_____

_____

_____

_____

_____

_____

_____

_____

The Gift of Obedience

SCRIPTURE

"If you love me, keep my commands."
— John 14:15 (NIV)

DEVOTIONAL

Obedience isn't about earning God's love—it's our response to it. Trusting His way, even when it's not easy or popular, brings life, peace, and purpose.

Every act of obedience draws you closer to His heart and aligns you with His best for you.

Sometimes obedience requires stepping out of your comfort zone or standing firm when others take a different path. But God's way is always worth it.

When you choose to obey, you open the door for God's blessings and guidance to flow freely in your life.

Remember, obedience isn't about perfection—it's about faithfulness. Each step you take in trust is a step toward the abundant life He promises.

PRAYER

Jesus, help me obey You out of love, not obligation. Give me the courage to follow where You lead, even when it's hard. Let my obedience be a reflection of my trust in You. Amen.

REFLECTION

Is there something God's asking you to obey that feels difficult? How has obedience to God brought blessing in your life before? What does loving God through obedience look like in your daily life?

_____

_____

_____

_____

_____

_____

_____

_____

_____

_____

_____

Choose Community

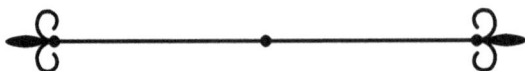

SCRIPTURE

"As iron sharpens iron, so one person sharpens another." — Proverbs 27:17 (NIV)

DEVOTIONAL

You weren't meant to do life alone. Community sharpens you, challenges you, and helps you grow. Surround yourself with people who encourage your faith, not compromise it.

In college, work, or new cities, be intentional about finding godly friends who speak truth and walk beside you.

True friendship isn't just about fun—it's about accountability, support, and spiritual growth. Friends who pray with you, listen to you, and lovingly point you back to God are priceless.

Don't be afraid to seek out mentors or join groups where you can connect with others who share your values and vision.

Remember, iron sharpens iron—choose relationships that sharpen your faith and help you become the person God created you to be.

PRAYER

God, thank You for the gift of community. Lead me to people who build me up in faith, and help me to be that kind of friend to others. Amen.

REFLECTION

Who are your "iron sharpens iron" people? Are there relationships you need to strengthen—or release? How can you be a godly friend to others?

_____

_____

_____

_____

_____

_____

_____

_____

_____

_____

_____

_____

_____

_____

Trust Over Control

SCRIPTURE

"Trust in the Lord with all your heart and lean not on your own understanding..." — Proverbs 3:5 (NIV)

DEVOTIONAL

We all like to feel in control—but trust means surrendering that control to God. It means choosing His wisdom over your own understanding, even when it doesn't make sense.

Let go of the pressure to figure everything out. God is trustworthy, even when you can't see the whole picture.

Sometimes the hardest part of faith is letting go of the need to have all the answers and simply resting in God's goodness.

When you surrender your plans and fears to Him, you open yourself to His perfect peace—a peace that surpasses all understanding.

Remember, God's timing and ways are higher than ours. Trusting Him doesn't mean the path is easy, but it means you never walk it alone.

Lean into His promises, knowing that He is faithful to guide, provide, and carry you through every uncertainty.

PRAYER

Lord, I surrender my plans and my need for control. Teach me to trust You with all my heart and to follow where You lead. Amen.

REFLECTION

What area of your life are you trying to control right now? How can you practice surrender in that area? What would it look like to fully trust God this week?

_____

_____

_____

_____

_____

_____

_____

_____

_____

_____

_____

_____

_____

You Are Sent

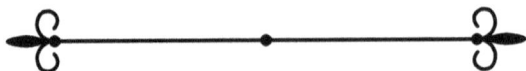

SCRIPTURE

"As the Father has sent me, I am sending you."
— John 20:21b (NIV)

DEVOTIONAL

Graduation isn't just the end of something—it's the beginning of being sent. You're stepping into the world as God's ambassador, not just as a student or employee, but as a light bearer.

Every classroom, office, or friend group is a mission field. You don't have to go far to make an eternal impact.

God calls you to live with purpose and intentionality wherever you are—your daily life is a chance to show His love and truth.

You carry the hope of Christ in your words, actions, and attitude. Even small acts of kindness or moments of courage can open hearts and change lives.

Remember, being sent means being ready— ready to serve, to love, and to reflect God's light in a world that desperately needs it.

So step forward boldly, knowing that God has equipped you and sent you exactly where you are meant to be.

PRAYER

Jesus, thank You for sending me with purpose. Help me to live boldly, love well, and reflect You in every space I enter. Amen.

REFLECTION

Where is God sending you right now? How can you live as His representative in your everyday life? What does it mean to live on mission where you are?

_____

_____

_____

_____

_____

_____

_____

_____

_____

_____

_____

Let Go of Comparison

SCRIPTURE

"Let us run with perseverance the race marked out for us…" — Hebrews 12:1b (NIV)

DEVOTIONAL

Comparison is a thief—of joy, peace, and focus. It distracts you from your own race by pulling your eyes to someone else's. But God has marked out your race, uniquely designed for you.

Run it with perseverance. Trust that He knows what He's doing in your story, even if it looks different from someone else's.

When you compare yourself to others, you miss the beautiful ways God is working uniquely in your life. Your journey has a purpose and timing that only He understands.

Focus on the gifts, opportunities, and lessons He's given you, and celebrate the progress you've made, no matter how small it seems.

Remember, success isn't about outpacing others—it's about faithfully running your own race with integrity and joy. God's plan for you is perfect, and He's cheering you on every step of the way.

PRAYER

God, help me stay in my lane and trust Your timing. Free me from the need to compare and give me confidence in the story You're writing in my life. Amen.

REFLECTION

In what ways are you tempted to compare your journey to others'? How can you stay focused on the race God has marked out for you? What does it look like to celebrate others without losing your joy?

_____

_____

_____

_____

_____

_____

_____

_____

_____

_____

_____

When You Don't Know What's Next

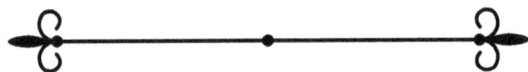

SCRIPTURE

"Your word is a lamp to my feet and a light for my path." — Psalm 119:105 (NIV)

DEVOTIONAL

You may not have a five-year plan—and that's okay. God rarely shows us the whole path at once. He gives us just enough light for the next step. Faith isn't about having all the answers; it's about trusting the One who does. When you're unsure what's next, stay close to the light.

It's natural to want clarity and direction, but sometimes God's timing and plans unfold in ways we don't expect. Instead of stressing over the unknown, lean into His presence.

Take each day as it comes, trusting that He is guiding your footsteps, even when the road ahead is unclear.

Remember, Jesus said, "I am the light of the world" (John 8:12). As long as you stay close to Him, you'll never walk in darkness, no matter how uncertain the path may seem.

PRAYER

Lord, I don't need to know the whole path—just the next step. Lead me with Your Word and give me the courage to follow You, one step at a time. Amen.

REFLECTION

What decisions or unknowns are weighing on you right now? How can God's Word guide your next step? What's one small act of obedience you can take today?

_____

_____

_____

_____

_____

_____

_____

_____

_____

_____

_____

He Will Finish What He Started

SCRIPTURE

"He who began a good work in you will carry it on to completion..." — Philippians 1:6a (NIV)

DEVOTIONAL

Graduation marks the completion of a chapter, but not the story. God is still writing it, and He's not done.

What He started in your heart—the dreams, the growth, the transformation—He will continue. You don't have to finish the work alone. He's faithful to complete what He begins.

Sometimes it's easy to feel like the finish line is the end, but God sees beyond what you can. He's already working on the next chapters of your life, filled with purpose and promise.

Trust that His plan is bigger than your plans and that He will equip you for every step ahead.

Lean into His faithfulness and grace, knowing that the best is yet to come because He who began a good work in you will carry it on to completion (Philippians 1:6).

PRAYER

God, thank You for beginning a good work in me.
I trust You to keep writing my story. When I feel
unfinished, remind me that You are still working.
Amen.

REFLECTION

What "good work" has God begun in you? Where do
you feel stuck or unfinished? How can you rest in
the promise that God isn't done with you?

_____

_____

_____

_____

_____

_____

_____

_____

_____

_____

Success Redefined

"What good is it for someone to gain the whole world, yet forfeit their soul?" — Mark 8:36 (NIV)

DEVOTIONAL

The world defines success by titles, money, and followers. But God defines success by faithfulness, obedience, and love.

You could gain every worldly achievement and still feel empty. True success is becoming who God created you to be and living with purpose that glorifies Him.

Success in God's eyes isn't about how many people know your name, but about how deeply you know and follow Him. It's about living with integrity, serving others, and reflecting Christ's love in all you do.

When you prioritize God's approval over the world's applause, you'll find a fulfillment and peace that no trophy or paycheck can provide.

Remember, the greatest success story is the one written by God's hand as you walk faithfully in His calling, one step at a time.

PRAYER

Lord, help me pursue Your definition of success. Teach me to value faithfulness over fame and purpose over popularity. I want to honor You in all I do. Amen.

REFLECTION

What does success mean to you? Are you chasing God's approval or the world's? How can you redefine success in your current season?

_____

_____

_____

_____

_____

_____

_____

_____

_____

_____

_____

Take Every Thought Captive

SCRIPTURE

"We take captive every thought to make it obedient to Christ." — 2 Corinthians 10:5b (NIV)

DEVOTIONAL

Your mind is a battlefield, and not every thought that enters belongs there. Some thoughts bring fear, doubt, or insecurity. But God gives you authority to take those captive and replace them with His truth. What you dwell on shapes how you live. Speak truth to your thoughts, and let God's Word lead your thinking.

Negative thoughts can sneak in quietly, but they don't have to have the final say. You have the power through Christ to reject lies and embrace God's promises.

When worry, fear, or self-doubt start to rise, pause and remind yourself of who God says you are—loved, chosen, capable, and strong.

Fill your mind with Scripture, prayer, and positive affirmations rooted in God's truth. Over time, your thought life will transform, helping you walk in confidence and peace.

Remember, renewing your mind is a daily battle,

but with God's help, victory is yours.

PRAYER

Father, help me take every thought captive and make it obedient to Christ. Replace fear with faith, lies with truth, and doubt with confidence in You. Amen.

REFLECTION

What negative thoughts do you struggle with? How can you replace those with Scripture? What would it look like to think with a renewed mind?

_____

_____

_____

_____

_____

_____

_____

_____

_____

_____

You're Never Too Young

SCRIPTURE

"Don't let anyone look down on you because you are young…" — 1 Timothy 4:12a (NIV)

DEVOTIONAL

Age doesn't limit God's calling. All through Scripture, He used young people—David, Esther, Jeremiah—to do mighty things.

Don't wait until you feel "ready." If God is calling you, He will equip you. Your voice matters. Your faith matters. Your courage can lead others.

Sometimes the world tells you to wait your turn, to earn more experience, or to hold back until you feel prepared. But God often chooses to work powerfully through those who are willing, regardless of age.

Your passion, energy, and fresh perspective are valuable tools God can use to make a difference. Trust Him to guide you step by step and provide what you need along the way.

Remember, God's strength is made perfect in our weakness (2 Corinthians 12:9). When you say "yes" to His call, He shows up in ways you never imagined.

Step out in faith, knowing that your youth is not a limitation but a platform for God's purpose.

PRAYER

God, thank You for choosing and using me now. Help me lead by example and live boldly in the calling You've placed on my life—no matter my age. Amen.

REFLECTION

Have you ever felt "too young" or unqualified for something? What's one way you can be an example in your youth? How has God already used you at your age?

_____

_____

_____

_____

_____

_____

_____

_____

_____

Run from Temptation

SCRIPTURE

"Flee the evil desires of youth and pursue righteousness, faith, love and peace…"
— 2 Timothy 2:22a (NIV)

DEVOTIONAL

Temptation isn't a sign of weakness—it's part of life. But how you respond to it shapes your character. God doesn't call you to fight temptation alone—He tells you to flee.

Running from temptation isn't cowardly; it's wisdom. And running toward God gives you strength. Temptation often comes disguised as something harmless or appealing, but it can quickly pull you away from God's best for your life. Recognizing the danger and choosing to turn away takes courage and trust.

God provides the tools you need—His Word, prayer, and the Holy Spirit's power—to resist and overcome. When you flee temptation, you're not just avoiding danger; you're actively protecting your heart and future.

Remember, every time you choose to run toward God instead of temptation, you build spiritual strength and deepen your relationship with Him. You are growing into the person God created you to be—strong, wise, and victorious.

PRAYER

Lord, give me the wisdom to flee temptation and the strength to pursue what's right. Help me crave what brings life, not destruction. Amen.

REFLECTION

What temptations are most present in your life right now? What does "fleeing" look like practically in those areas? Who can help hold you accountable?

_____

_____

_____

_____

_____

_____

_____

_____

_____

_____

_____

Keep Dreaming with God

SCRIPTURE

"Now to him who is able to do immeasurably more than all we ask or imagine..." — Ephesians 3:20 (NIV)

DEVOTIONAL

God is the ultimate dream-giver. He's not intimidated by your big dreams—or your small ones. But He also invites you into dreams that are bigger than you, because they require Him.

Don't stop dreaming with God. Let your imagination be fueled by faith, not fear.

Sometimes dreams feel too big, too impossible, or too risky. But that's where God's power shines brightest—when we step out beyond what we can do on our own.

When you dream with God, you're partnering with the Creator of the universe, who can turn the impossible into reality. He gives you the vision and the strength to pursue what matters most.

So hold onto your dreams tightly, but hold onto God even tighter. Let His Spirit inspire your goals and give you courage to keep moving forward, even when the path is unclear.

Remember, with God, no dream is too big, and

no step of faith is wasted.

PRAYER

Father, thank You for being a God of big dreams. Help me dream with You and trust You with the details. Do more than I can imagine—for Your glory. Amen.

REFLECTION

What dreams has God placed on your heart? Do your dreams leave room for God to work beyond your ability? How can you pursue those dreams with courage?

_____

_____

_____

_____

_____

_____

_____

_____

_____

_____

Rest Is Not a Weakness

SCRIPTURE

"Come to me, all you who are weary and burdened, and I will give you rest." — Matthew 11:28 (NIV)

DEVOTIONAL

Rest isn't laziness. It's obedience. God designed rhythms of rest to protect your soul and remind you that the world doesn't rest on your shoulders—it rests in His hands.

In a world that glorifies hustle, choose rest. Let your identity be found in being God's child, not just in doing for Him.

You were not created to run on empty. Even Jesus took time to withdraw, to pray, and to rest. Rest is not weakness—it's wisdom. It's a declaration that your worth isn't based on how much you produce, achieve, or accomplish.

When you pause, you make space to hear God more clearly, to be refreshed, and to remember who holds everything together. Rest re-centers your heart and renews your strength.

So take a breath. Lay down the pressure to constantly perform. God is more interested in your presence than your productivity. He invites you to come to Him and find true rest—not just for your body, but for your soul (Matthew 11:28).

PRAYER

Jesus, thank You for inviting me to rest. Help me to slow down and trust that You're in control. Refresh my soul as I find peace in You. Amen.

REFLECTION

Do you view rest as necessary or optional? What would it look like to create healthy rhythms of rest? How does resting remind you of your dependence on God?

_____

_____

_____

_____

_____

_____

_____

_____

_____

_____

The Influence of Your Life

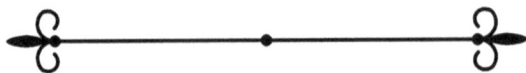

SCRIPTURE

"Let your light shine before others, that they may see your good deeds and glorify your Father in heaven." — Matthew 5:16 (NIV)

DEVOTIONAL

Your life tells a story—every word, action, and decision. People are watching, even when you don't realize it. Let your life reflect Christ so clearly that others are drawn to Him.

You don't have to be loud to be influential. Just be faithful.

The way you treat people, how you respond under pressure, and what you prioritize all speak louder than you might think. You may never know who's being encouraged by your quiet consistency, your kindness, or your commitment to what's right.

God isn't looking for perfection—He's looking for a willing heart. Your ordinary, everyday choices have eternal impact when they're surrendered to Him.

So keep showing up with integrity. Keep loving well. Keep standing firm in your faith. You don't have to shine a spotlight on yourself; just live in a way that shines His light.

Your faithfulness plants seeds—some you'll see grow, and some you won't. But trust that God is using your life as a testimony of His grace.

PRAYER

Lord, let my life point others to You. Help me live with intentionality and integrity so others can see Your love through me. Amen.

REFLECTION

What story is your life telling right now? How can you shine brighter in your everyday actions? Who's someone you influence—whether you realize it or not?

_____

_____

_____

_____

_____

_____

_____

_____

Forgiveness Frees You

SCRIPTURE

"Forgive as the Lord forgave you."
— Colossians 3:13b (NIV)

DEVOTIONAL

Holding onto unforgiveness only chains you to the pain. Forgiveness doesn't mean what happened was okay—it means you're choosing to let God handle justice.

When you forgive, you free your heart to heal. And when you remember how much you've been forgiven, it becomes easier to extend that grace. Forgiveness isn't about forgetting—it's about surrendering. It's choosing to let go of the need to get even and trusting God to be the righteous Judge. Carrying bitterness only weighs you down and keeps you stuck in the past.

God calls us to forgive not to minimize our hurt, but to protect our hearts. He knows that unforgiveness can harden us, but forgiveness makes space for freedom and peace.

Remember, forgiveness is not a one-time feeling—it's a decision, sometimes daily, to release the offense and trust God with the outcome.

You are never more like Jesus than when you choose to forgive, even when it's hard. And in doing so, you open your heart to experience the same healing grace He has so freely given to you.

PRAYER

God, help me forgive as You've forgiven me. Free me from bitterness and help me walk in grace and healing. I trust You with the pain. Amen.

REFLECTION

Is there someone you need to forgive? How has unforgiveness impacted your heart? What would it feel like to release that to God?

_____

_____

_____

_____

_____

_____

_____

_____

_____

Be Faithful in the Little Things

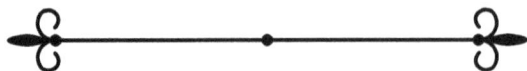

SCRIPTURE

"Whoever can be trusted with very little can also be trusted with much..." — Luke 16:10a (NIV)

DEVOTIONAL

The little things matter. Faithfulness in the unseen prepares you for the spotlight. God often tests our character in quiet places before He opens doors to bigger ones.

Be diligent where you are. Show up, do the work, and stay faithful. Promotion comes from God. It's easy to crave recognition or dream of influence, but God is more concerned with who you're becoming than where you're going. The small, everyday choices—how you handle responsibilities, how you treat people when no one is watching, how you respond when things don't go your way—are shaping the foundation of your future.

Jesus said those who are faithful with little can be trusted with much (Luke 16:10). That means your current season, no matter how ordinary it feels, is significant in His eyes. He sees your quiet commitment, your unseen efforts, and your integrity behind the scenes.

God's timing is perfect, and when you're ready, He'll open the right doors. Until then, be excellent where you are. Don't despise small beginnings— God often does His deepest work there. Trust that He's building something lasting through your daily faithfulness.

PRAYER

Lord, help me be faithful in the little things. Teach me to honor You in what seems small, trusting You with what's ahead. Amen.

REFLECTION

What "small" assignment has God given you right now? How can you be more faithful where you are? Are you willing to grow in the quiet before you lead in the public?

_____

_____

_____

_____

_____

_____

_____

Stay Humble and Teachable

SCRIPTURE

"God opposes the proud but shows favor to the humble." — James 4:6b (NIV)

DEVOTIONAL

Humility isn't thinking less of yourself—it's thinking of yourself less and recognizing your need for God and others.

A humble heart attracts God's favor and keeps you grounded when success comes. As you step into new opportunities and experiences, it can be tempting to rely solely on your own knowledge, gifts, or achievements. But the most powerful leaders are those who never stop learning—who know they still have room to grow.

Teachability is a sign of wisdom. It means being open to correction, willing to listen, and ready to admit when you're wrong. It's also a reminder that no matter how far you've come, you still need God's guidance every step of the way.

Humility draws people in, while pride pushes them away. It keeps you rooted in truth and reminds you that all you have—your gifts, your growth, your influence—is from God.

Stay teachable, and you'll stay in position for God to continue shaping you into who He's called you to be.

PRAYER

God, keep my heart humble and teachable. Help me to seek wisdom, learn from others, and always depend on You. Amen.

REFLECTION

How do you respond to correction or feedback? Are there areas where pride is sneaking in? What's one way you can grow in humility this week?

_____

_____

_____

_____

_____

_____

_____

_____

_____

God Is Your Provider

SCRIPTURE

"And my God will meet all your needs according to the riches of his glory in Christ Jesus."
— Philippians 4:19 (NIV)

DEVOTIONAL

As you step into adulthood, financial needs, job uncertainties, and future questions can feel overwhelming. But God is not just your Savior—He's also your Provider. He promises to meet your needs—not always your wants, but always in a way that shapes your faith and reveals His care.

You may not always know how everything will work out, but God does. Provision might look like a part-time job, a generous friend, a timely opportunity, or simply peace when you need it most. It may not be flashy, but it's always faithful.

Your job is to trust and obey—work hard, steward well, and keep your heart fixed on Him. His job is to provide what you truly need, right on time. He's not just preparing the path ahead of you—He's walking it with you.

PRAYER

Lord, I trust You to provide what I need today and tomorrow. Help me to rely on You, not my own efforts or fears. You are faithful. Amen.

REFLECTION

In what areas do you need to trust God's provision? How has God provided for you in the past? What does trusting His provision look like practically?

_____

_____

_____

_____

_____

_____

_____

_____

_____

_____

_____

Walk in the Spirit

SCRIPTURE

"Since we live by the Spirit, let us keep in step with the Spirit." — Galatians 5:25 (NIV)

DEVOTIONAL

Walking with God is a daily journey of staying in rhythm with the Holy Spirit—listening, responding, and obeying His gentle nudges.
It's less about perfection and more about direction. God isn't expecting you to have flawless days—He's inviting you to walk closely with Him, one step at a time.

In a world that moves fast and demands instant decisions, it's easy to rush ahead or feel pressure to always "get it right." But the Spirit often speaks in whispers, not shouts. He leads through peace, not panic. When your heart is tuned to His, you'll sense when to pause, when to act, and when to wait.

Staying in step with God requires intentionality—quiet moments in prayer, space to listen, and a heart ready to follow. Don't worry if you miss it sometimes. Just keep returning to Him. He's not measuring your pace; He's inviting you to walk in His presence.

Let your decisions flow from peace, not pressure. Let your life move in rhythm with His grace.

PRAYER

Holy Spirit, lead me today. Help me stay in step with You and trust Your guidance. Tune my heart to hear Your voice above all others. Amen.

REFLECTION

How do you recognize the Spirit's leading in your life? Are there areas where you've rushed ahead or fallen behind? What's one step of obedience you can take today?

_____

_____

_____

_____

_____

_____

_____

_____

_____

Don't Fear Failure

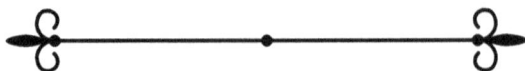

SCRIPTURE

"Though he may stumble, he will not fall, for the Lord upholds him with his hand." — Psalm 37:24 (NIV)

DEVOTIONAL

Failure isn't the end—it's often the classroom where God teaches, shapes, and strengthens you. You're going to mess up. You'll take wrong turns. You'll make choices you wish you hadn't. But none of that disqualifies you from God's purpose. In fact, some of the deepest growth happens in the aftermath of a fall.

God doesn't waste your failures. He uses them to develop humility, deepen your dependence on Him, and refine your character. His hand never lets go, even when you feel like you've let Him down. Grace means you don't have to earn your way back—you just have to turn back.

Your worth isn't in your performance—it's in His grace. You're not loved more on your best day or less on your worst. So when you fall, fall forward—toward the God who restores, redeems, and rewrites your story with hope.

PRAYER

Father, thank You that failure doesn't define me—
You do. When I stumble, lift me up. Help me learn,
grow, and keep moving forward with You. Amen.

REFLECTION

What failure are you afraid of? How has God used
past mistakes for growth? What truth can you cling
to when you stumble?

_____

_____

_____

_____

_____

_____

_____

_____

_____

_____

_____

Your Identity Is in Christ

SCRIPTURE

"Therefore, if anyone is in Christ, the new creation has come..." — 2 Corinthians 5:17 (NIV)

DEVOTIONAL

You'll be tempted to define yourself by your GPA, your career, your relationships, or your accomplishments.

The world will try to label you—by success, by failure, by what you do or don't have. But all those things are temporary. They change. They rise and fall. Your true identity isn't in a title, a trophy, or someone else's approval. It's unshakable, and it's rooted in Christ.

You are chosen, loved, forgiven, and called. You are not what you've done—you are who God says you are. In Christ, you are a new creation, set apart for a purpose that goes far deeper than achievements.

When everything around you shifts—your plans, your path, your performance—this truth remains: you belong to Him. Let His voice be louder than the noise. Let His love define your worth. You don't have to earn what He's already given you—just receive it, and live from it.

PRAYER

Jesus, remind me that my identity is in You, not in what I do or what others say. Help me live boldly as a new creation, secure in Your love. Amen.

REFLECTION

What are you tempted to let define your identity? What does it mean to you that you're a new creation in Christ? How can you live confidently in who God says you are?

_____

_____

_____

_____

_____

_____

_____

_____

_____

_____

Keep Your Eyes on Eternity

"Set your minds on things above, not on earthly things." — Colossians 3:2 (NIV)

DEVOTIONAL

It's easy to get caught up in temporary things—grades, jobs, opinions, trends. But you were made for more.

The world around you constantly pulls your attention toward what's fleeting and often shallow. It can feel like success is measured by popularity, possessions, or status. But those things don't last—and they don't satisfy the deepest parts of your soul.

When you live with eternity in mind, your perspective changes. Suddenly, what truly matters becomes clear. You begin to value people over prestige, seeing each person as someone God loves deeply. Purpose takes priority over popularity, guiding your choices and giving your life meaning beyond momentary applause. And above all, God's kingdom becomes your ultimate goal—His plans over your own desires.

This doesn't mean ignoring the present or your responsibilities. It means letting God's eternal perspective shape how you live every day. When you do, your priorities become anchored in what lasts forever, and your heart finds lasting peace.

PRAYER

Lord, help me fix my eyes on what matters most. Let my life reflect eternal values, not temporary rewards. Keep my heart focused on You. Amen.

REFLECTION

What "earthly things" distract you most? How can you live today with eternity in view? What small decisions can have eternal impact?

_____

_____

_____

_____

_____

_____

_____

_____

A Life That Soars

SCRIPTURE

"But those who hope in the Lord will renew their strength. They will soar on wings like eagles…"
— Isaiah 40:31a (NIV)

DEVOTIONAL

You were created to soar—not in your own strength, but in His.

Life will bring winds of resistance—challenges that try to hold you down, doubts that whisper you can't, and obstacles that seem too big. But when God is your foundation, you're anchored in something far stronger than circumstances or feelings.

With Him, you won't just survive the storms—you'll rise above them. His power will lift you higher than you thought possible. So when fear or fatigue threatens to clip your wings, remember: your strength comes from the One who gave you breath.

Keep hoping when the path is unclear. Keep trusting when the road gets rough. Keep walking step by step, knowing that your story is just beginning. With God guiding your flight, it will be full of purpose, impact, and breathtaking heights.

PRAYER

God, I put my hope in You. Teach me to rise above fear, doubt, and weariness. Let my life soar—not for my glory, but for Yours. Amen.

REFLECTION

Where in your life do you need renewed strength? What does soaring in God's strength look like for you? How has your hope grown in this journey?

_____

_____

_____

_____

_____

_____

_____

_____

_____

_____

_____

_____

_____

Closing Thoughts

You made it to the end of this devotional journey—but this is only the beginning of the story God is writing with your life.

Over the past 52 weeks, you've reflected, prayed, grown, and hopefully come to know God more personally and deeply. You've faced real-life questions, wrestled with truth, and discovered that courage doesn't always look like bold moves or loud declarations—sometimes it looks like quiet obedience, honest faith, and small steps in the right direction.

As you continue forward, remember:

- You don't have to soar every single day.
- Some days you'll walk. Some days you'll wait.
- But even in the waiting, God is working.

Keep building your life on God's Word.
Keep seeking His voice above the noise.
And keep trusting that He who began a good work in you will carry it to completion.
You were made to soar—not in your own strength, but in His.
So go forward with courage.

Go forward with faith.

Go forward with the unshakable truth that the God who goes before you is also the One who walks beside you.

NOW—GO CHANGE THE WORLD.

About the Author

Rebecca graduated from Malone College in 2008 with a Bachelor's degree in Youth Ministry. She started writing & illustrating in 2013, about her dog Pookie, when she wanted a fun and wholesome story for her nieces and nephews, some of which were learning to read. She plans to keep up her series and write others. In 2019, she launched a publishing and entertainment company to help kids explore and nurture their creative side through books, tv shows, and art classes.

Along with *The Adventures of Pookie* children's book series, she is the illustrator of her sister, Megan Yee's books in the God's Books series. She is also the author of the personal development book *The Creative Minds Guide to Success*. She travels full time in a 5th wheel RV with her husband Eric, and their dog, Bailey, for his job as a Journeyman Lineman and writes about their adventures along the way.

Check out more:

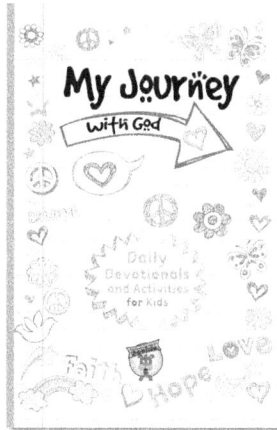

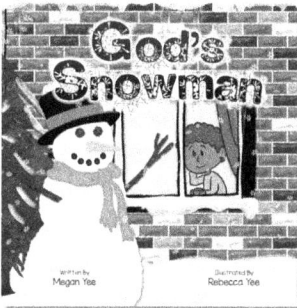

God's Masterpiece

My Journey with God
Daily Devotionals and Activities for Kids

God's Little Pumpkin
Megan Yee   Rebecca Yee

God's Snowman
Written by Megan Yee
Illustrated by Rebecca Yee

Love, Jesus

AdventuresOfPookie.com

The Adventures of Pookie

ENTERTAINMENT

Books   Shows   Classes

www.ingramcontent.com/pod-product-compliance
Lightning Source LLC
Chambersburg PA
CBHW071946100426
42736CB00042B/2220